BORDERLESS TRADE

BORDERLESS TRADE

A STEP-BY-STEP GUIDE TO EXPORTING YOUR PRODUCT

OLORI BOYE-AJAYI

BORDERLESS TRADE
A Step-by-Step Guide To Exporting Your Product

FIRST EDITION

Copyright © 2020 by Olori Boye-Ajayi

All rights reserved. No part of this publication may be reproduced, stored in a retrieval system or transmitted, in any form or by any means, electronic, mechanical, photocopying, recording or otherwise, without the written permission of the publisher.

Written permission must be secured from the publisher to use or reproduce any part of this book except for brief quotations in reviews or articles.

Editing, Design and Layout
Levionlinepublishing@gmail.com

For more information about this book and the author contact hello@theark.company

TABLE OF CONTENTS

Chapter One	Piece Of Cake Or Not? Is Export Really For You?	8
Chapter Two	Understanding The Markets Available	15
Chapter Three	Developing Your Export Plan	21
Chapter Four	Pitfalls To Avoid	35
Chapter Five	Frequently Asked Questions	51
Closing Words		65

Chapter One

PIECE OF CAKE OR NOT?
IS EXPORT REALLY FOR YOU?

You most likely purchased this guide because you are interested in exporting your products, services, knowledge, or skill to other countries or, at least, want to know what the process would entail. For some, maybe you're looking for a way to grow your business, or you've received an inquiry from a prospective customer in another country.

Jumping into markets unprepared will cost you time and money and, worst of all, may damage the reputation of your business. This is why I wrote this book – for you not to waste your time. You will learn about mistakes to avoid on your export journey.

If you are eager to sell your products into new markets or are hesitant about exporting because it seems overwhelming and confusing. whether you are at one end of the spectrum or the other or anywhere in between, this guide is a useful tool for you!

This guide has been tailored to small businesses which may not have the resources or the capacity to approach exporting in the same way a larger business might. I hope to make the steps to exporting clear and easy to understand, and inspire you to begin putting measures in place that will help to ensure your export success.

A lot of people tell me during my business coaching sessions, "Olori, I want to scale up," and one of the quickest ways to do this is to export; sell your product in other regions. It's a no-brainer.

However, successful exporting requires your time, resources, and knowledge to prepare your products and staff for a foreign marketplace, to identify specific opportunities, and to maximize the potential of a successful venture.

This title is a series of different editions, this being the first. This edition will guide through what you need to know, your export plan, understanding how to choose export destinations, and many more gems.

The second edition will take you through logistic and freight options, export pricing, how to set up your international payments, how to source for buyers, technical documentation and legal processes required.

WHAT IS AN EXPORT?

As a basic definition, any movement of goods, services, knowledge outside of the country is considered an export. You can be a commodity exporter, merchant exporter, or manufacturing exporter.

The differences between each will be explained to you in a chapter on Frequently Asked Questions. Also, by the end of this book, you will understand and have a list of resources to help start the export journey.

The information shared will link your business to a world of opportunities. You can succeed in the global marketplace once you know how to play in it.

WHY SHOULD I CONSIDER EXPORTING?
There are many reasons to export. The first being, there is export potential in each person's business. An obvious benefit of exporting is that it offers a means to increasing sales by taking advantage of global demand. But the benefits of exporting do not end there:

- Exporting provides an opportunity to specialize in areas in which you are the most competitive by providing access to a larger customer base. In times where your base of operation is no longer yielding what you would desire, consider other product offerings from your product mix. You can also modify your existing product and offer it another market.
- Exporting helps to reduce the risks of economic downturns by spreading risk across markets.
- Exporting enables your business to earn valuable foreign exchange.
- Exporting helps to boost the competitiveness of your business in both domestic and

foreign markets through exposure to new ideas and processes.
- Exporting allows your business safeguard itself from the threats of operating in one market. For example, ZARA stores in Italy may be hit during a economic downturn while ZARA in Singapore might be booming due to increased consumer spending trends.

A helpful tool I highly recommend in assessing your export readiness and determining whether exporting is right for your business is a SWOT analysis.

As some of you may know, SWOT stands for 'Strengths, Weaknesses, Opportunities, Threats'. This analysis provides a bird's eye view of the key factors necessary in making business decisions.

A SWOT analysis can be used to help answer the question, 'Should I go into export?' or in more specifically, 'Should my company export leather handbags to the United States?'

I have included a SWOT template at the end of the book to answer what I call an export SWOT analysis. It will really help you navigate your thoughts and, most likely, answer questions you're unsure about.

Chapter Two

UNDERSTANDING THE MARKETS AVAILABLE

To develop your export business into a successful one, the first thing to consider is AVAILABLE MARKETS. You must ensure you understand your target market(s); this involves conducting a research on your export destination(s). It's a very insightful step and can really open you up to other opportunities available in different parts of the world; even the ones you haven't visited yet. Your products can go ahead of you and make you money.

In order to make a well-rounded decision on how to proceed on the export journey, you should know there are two key types of market research: primary research (market intelligence) and secondary research (market information).

Though it may seem counterintuitive, you should begin your market research efforts by undertaking secondary research. Once you have a good general understanding of your potential target markets, narrow them down by establishing the best fit for your business through primary research. Your research allows you to conduct a comprehensive market analysis like identification of promising markets, analysing trade flows, identifying and calculating import tariffs / duties, defining and comparing international standards, and much more.

Don't get overwhelmed, there are several free tools for conducting your market analysis. These tools will enhance your understanding of your target market(s). You can find these tools via the link I have shared below.

Take your time at this stage. What you uncover will inform your next steps and how well prepared you are. Remember, nobody likes unpleasant surprises; so, the more you know, the better equipped you are when making vital decisions.

http://www.intracen.org/itc/market-info-tools/market-analysis-studies/

If you don't know what to look for, start by answering these questions through your research and put your answers in a file you can refer to later.

- What is the demand or export potential of your product in international markets?
- Have you identified a market for your product?
- What are the options for entering the preferred market?
- Will your product be accepted in its current form or will you have to repackage it to meet international standards?

When the market research is complete, contact some of the businesses or platforms you found by offering them a free sample of your product. Taking this step means you've uncovered the main competitors in what you're offering.

HOW ELSE CAN I FIND A BUYER?

I have listed some international and local buyers who you should check out over a glass of your favourite drink in the second edition of this book. It's a treasure chest.

Acquaint yourself with company names, do further research on LinkedIn on the procurement or buying team, and reach out to them with a sales pitch they could never refuse. However, I have listed a very good resource within this book also.

Chapter Three

DEVELOPING YOUR EXPORT PLAN

So many things and ideas will pop up during your market research. It could unravel new terrains that you can service alongside your initial product if it requires the same supply chain.

For example, you make womenswear with cotton plain fabric, and at some point during your research you discover that men's undergarments are in shortage in Kenya. That might be an additional market you want to add.

In order to ensure you have your ideas and business goals all tied together without a fragmented plan, you must develop your export plan (EP). This is an essential piece of the whole export puzzle. You can have a skeletal framework of what you want to achieve and what might be required to achieve it.

An export plan is not a stand-alone document. It should be developed in the context of your business plan. If you do not have a business plan or have not updated your business plan in years, take some time to develop or update it now.

Your EP must be revised as you go along in the export journey; you will find better ways of doing things once the ball is rolling. Be flexible with your EP.

A complete export plan includes:

- Best market selection and segment
- Definition of your unique value proposition (What do you offer? What makes you different from your competitors?)
- Selection of the best distribution channel (distributors, retailers, end users, etc.)
- Selection of promotional instruments (website, social media presence, brochures, catalogues, trade fairs, etc.)
- Selection of a competitive pricing mechanism

In summary, an export plan is a holding place for goals, market research, opportunities, decisions, resource requirements, and strategies.

Most importantly, it helps to answer the question, "Can we make money doing this?" Think of your export plan as a road map; it provides directions so a business can reach its destination in a direct manner, while avoiding detours and bumps in the road.

REGISTER WITH ASSOCIATIONS, AGENCIES, AND COUNCILS

One of the fastest ways to get a piece of the export pie with any product/service you might have is to join credible associations and forums and engage frequently with the members in it.

Getting buyers as an independent company can be stressful and a longer route before you get your first order. I strongly advise you sign up for one or more associations within your industry and, of course, export related associations and networks.

While registering for these, consider local and international options. While some may require you to pay a membership fee, see it as a token for entry into a bigger pool of opportunities.

Once you're in, follow the path of excellence in how you engage with the Presidents/EXCO members and sell your strengths and show a collaborative spirit; not competition or isolation. If you are shy and don't like to network, you will have to remove the shy cloak and immerse yourself in the opportunities presented in these agencies.

To guide your search on which associations to join, look for manufacturers' associations on a national level, export promotion councils for government, export advocacy programs by independent associations, or government selected agencies.

You will need to register your business with the necessary agency to get a license or exporters certificate which will be critical for buyers to know you have this basic requirement. Once registered, you will have access to numerous trainings and workshop and, in some cases, travel out on all-expense paid trade fairs where you can showcase your product.

Best of all, you begin to meet people just like yourself with humble beginnings, and you begin to share your export journey alongside good, bad, and not so pretty stories.

WOMEN IN EXPORT:
AN OVERLOOKED TALENT

One of my career highlights, and still is, is helping women entrepreneurs and business owners expand their businesses internationally. I saw a very unhealthy trend where reports show that women who run businesses are less likely to trade internationally than those owned by men. I wanted to help change the landscape for women, from being risk-averse to having the confidence to go for it, with the appropriate support.

Studies show that women-owned SMEs that export tend to earn more, pay more, employ more people, and be more productive than firms that only operate domestically. Yet, further studies show that only one in five exporting companies is owned by a woman, and that women-owned businesses are more likely to face obstacles to trade.

We have to take personal responsibility for our own products and services getting the global attention it deserves as female CEOs; the onus is on us.

It is more essential than ever for women business owners to be informed and inspired to grow globally. We need more development agencies and export councils to promote the women-in-export agenda.

Thanks to technology and the internet, even the smallest producer of goods and services can go global today by using global marketplaces such as EBay, which allows for fast, break-through growth, provided a business owner understands the know-how.

For the next 10 years, part of my goal is to strengthen women participation in the global economy and break down barriers preventing women from expanding their enterprises through exporting.

I have used Facebook to enjoin over 350 members in a small community of fashion and textile lovers which I started in 2015. This was my contribution in educating young business owners via weekly online classes on how to take a business global. I developed this into the mission of the company I founded, The Katie Wang Company.

In 2018, I self-funded weekly structured classes for women-owned businesses to educate them on the business of fashion. Besides passion, there is the business of the passion. The next step for us as a global company is to educate, and not just connect more young people, on the practical aspects of exporting, and provide them with concrete strategies for global entrepreneurship.

There are trade agencies, such as the International Trade Centre (ITC), which through the SheTrades initiative have over the years highlighted the significant role women play in development, moving from local business to global trade across various sectors. Many women have benefitted from exporting their hand-made or locally produced items and have not looked back since.

In your country of origin, search for women in export advocacy groups. In some cases, government tenders for manufacturing or other sector contracts are passed to these women before they make it to the general public.

Many agencies across the world have put women on the forefront of export trading. For instance, the SheTrades initiative supports Nigerian women through:

- Enabling market access
- Capacity building through training / webinars on the platform
- Taking advantage of trade and market tools
- Supporting women entrepreneurs to participate in annual global events
- On the spot registration on SheTrades initiative
- Additionally, it offers a digital platform (web and mobile app) for women entrepreneurs to connect to the international market.

I am deeply convinced that women are and can be important players in international trade at the service of development.

SUPPLY CHAIN MANAGEMENT

As an exporter to be, you must understand supply chain management and incorporate it into your export plan if the one you have currently doesn't fit the robust supply chain management system needed.

First things first, what is a supply chain? A supply chain is a network of facilities and distribution options that perform three primary functions:

- procurement of raw materials
- transformation of these materials into products, and
- distribution of these products to customers

Over the past 13 years, the International Trade Centre's Modular Learning System in Supply Chain Management (MLS-SCM) programme has helped train more than 30,000 business managers worldwide. Executives learn to manage the sourcing, movement, and storage of goods from source of production to point of consumption.

NEPC supports more than 2,000 women in exports. The council also facilitates capacity building opportunities for empowering women in trade.

SCM TRAINING PROGRAMME FOR EXPORTERS

For those new to supply chain management, the programme offers a complete range of courses, and for others who want to refresh or sharpen their skills, specialized courses are available. Participants can choose from more than 19 modules, study at their own pace, take exams, and gain internationally recognized professional certification.

The SCM programme consists of 19 modules covering key aspects of supply chain management including logistics, procurement, inventory management, as well as an independent training pack on SCM for SMEs.

It will be worth taking a look at what is being offered to women in export in your country on a local and national level. You may be pleasantly surprised. Some countries in state agencies ensure that women entrepreneurs have equal access to facilities to enhance their business.

NEPC created the Women in Export division to assist women through the following programs.

EXPORT TRAININGS/SEMINARS

- Zero-To-Export Training: an eight-week hands-on training programme to become ready for exports.
- Export Clinic: a one-day training covering the basics in exports for just starting exporters.

Participation is free, but there is a selection process. NEPC highly promotes women (interested) in exports to participate in these programmes. Find out the most up-to-date schedules and more information on these trainings in the event calendar.

Chapter Four

PITFALLS TO AVOID

While there are some stories I could share with you on times I failed in trying to navigate the export process, I'll share a particular scenario with you to buttress a point I intend to make.

When I started my export journey with ready-to-wear apparel for women, men, and children, I was so sure everything I needed was in place. I had beautiful designs, manufacturers, and, of course, was motivated by the fact that customers abroad were starting to inquire about our products. Little did I know, I wasn't half ready at the time.

The first customer order we ever got came from the United Kingdom for our womenswear selection. At the time, the unit prices were already set and things were ready as far as I was concerned. I had very little staff, about two people plus a driver. I was the marketer, the salesperson, the business development manager, the accountant and, of course, the CEO. That is the first pitfall I want to highlight before I continue.

You can't build your export business around yourself. it's not possible. You will make mistakes and be burnt out in no time. Between production, logistics, and customer relations, it's a lot! Get the staff you have up to speed on what needs to change in terms of standards, quality, and waste management at the beginning stages.

For this order, the customer requested for a total of 50 pieces at some point. We discussed via WhatsApp and she had pictures of the designs she had saved from different online marketplaces. Of course, when she asked "Can you create these designs?" My answer was "Yes!"

Mistake number two. Never say yes before you do a sampling and pattern process. I didn't have a pattern maker at the time; everything was done freehand. The customer didn't ask for a sample but asked for the next steps, which I was happy about. I felt she wasn't wasting any time (we all know customers who waste your time for one thing). I told her the next step was that I would send her an invoice. That was beginning of my many pitfalls.

Sending an invoice or payment for goods is step six from a customer inquiry. I skipped all of that just because I wanted to close the deal and make the sale in pounds sterling. Looking back now, I don't think I slept or chatted with anyone else because I really wanted to start exporting to the United Kingdom, after which I would then post the news on social media: We are now international! Wrong!

Never be in a hurry to close a deal you don't have the capacity to fulfil. Here's what you do after an inquiry. You inform the customer that their order is well received and you will get back to her within a few hours with information on design choices, quantity requested, and lead time. You shouldn't even discuss price at all at this stage except you already have this product in your offerings.

For a new item, price is determined after the sample has been agreed on by customer and seller; and even a lot can change between that time and production time.

Another mistake I made was that I didn't send a proper Order Request Form. Instead I used WhatsApp for our conversations, which was the beginning of my pricing and design problems. Chats were muddled up and I ended up giving the wrong prices to the items because they were just too many.

Remember, I just wanted to close the deal. So, I was willing to do anything to speed up the process, including allowing her negotiate my prices one by one. I'm actually laughing at myself right now as I remember this story.

You will need to put some structures in place, no matter how small it is you are starting out on your export journey. Have an order request form that all customers must fill before you take an order. This form must include basic information like a design ID, style description, sizes (put the options you produce here so it's not assumed that it is open), quantity and design in each size, any special requirement during and post production.

Finally, on your order request form ask for the delivery time, address (so you can start to get the delivery rates), contact person (in case you need to clarify some things stated in the form).

When I had received all her pictures and had given her wrong prices, I proceeded to send her the invoice. She asked why she had to pay 70% upfront. She claimed she didn't know me and it was a risk for her. So, I succumbed and asked her to pay 50% as we can't use our own money to produce her chosen items. She agreed.

I was so happy when she finally asked for my account details. The problem was I didn't have a UK business account. I couldn't believe this would be a stumbling block at this very crucial moment of closing this almost-done deal. I explained to her that we weren't registered in the UK (now the company is registered there) and all I could get her was a personal bank account.

She said this was getting funny because she expected we would have a more secure payment option. I thought she was being so difficult and probably just didn't want to pay. Now I agree with her.

Let me explain a few things at this point, the order request form allows you to do many things and get this process more standardized. When you receive an order, go through it with your staff (if you're a small business, do it yourself), your production manager or operations supervisor if you have one, and the person who will source and purchase the items.

When you've all agreed on clear terms, if you don't have existing supply, buy what it will take to make ONE product, not the full order. Never purchase raw materials for an order that is not confirmed by payment. I learnt this the hard way. In your bid to pleasing customers, don't start making a loss even before you get an order in.

After discussing the raw materials needed, go through the designs that the customer has chosen to see if it can be done by in-house staff. If it's a yes, then you're good to go with the pre-production sample. If you don't have the product in your current offering, you will have to bill the client for a pattern and a sample; but bill it all inclusive. In most countries, a sample is more expensive because of these factors.

For international payment solutions, there are several you can use if you don't have a bank account. Depending on where you are receiving money from, you will have to search for online, safe and secure options for your customers as you start your export business, and all these options should be in your export plan.

Customers will require a company account for payments as you grow bigger. There are some things you can get away with when you are small, but not when the big cats start ordering your products.

Another thing to clear up here is sometimes you will not be given a dime upfront due to some company policies on buying on credit or a product category being sold. You may have to wait 30 to 45 days after goods have arrived at the destination. It depends on the company's payment policy.

Always ask these questions on payment terms at the beginning. Don't assume a customer asking for your company account details means you are about to be paid. That invoice will go through their internal processes before the funds are released to you.

As you grow in the export space, you may require export financing which will help ease the burden of funding production of items in large orders. I cover more information on this in the second edition of this book.

In my story, when she eventually paid, I went straight into production with my manufacturers and that's when all the trouble began. We created no patterns and there was of course no standardization because of that. I divided the order across three manufacturers and each used their own patterns, or most likely freehand, in cutting the pattern.

Ten days later, I received all the items from each manufacturer and had 50 different looking items, even those in the same category. I was shaking in my boots. With shock and anger, I called the manufacturers to express my dissatisfaction and all they said was "Aunty, we made the items using the picture you sent us."

I was mortified because I had run out of cash from the clients' money. Remember, she had only paid 50%. So, I did what some people do, which is hope that the customer will not notice the errors. I packaged them, putting the better ones on top and the worse ones at the bottom, all the while hoping and wishing they would not inspect the items individually and notice the errors.

I sent the items to the customer's relative in my location who was supposed to get it across to my client. I called the customer to let her know we had delivered on time and the customer praised me for getting the items out within the agreed timeframe. I made no mention of the errors. Like I said, I hoped and prayed she would not notice the errors.

The following week, the client called me. I had missed her call. She called six times within the space of two minutes. When I saw the number of missed calls, I knew I was in trouble. I summoned the courage to call her back and was ready to hear her out.

As was expected, she hit me like a tonne of bricks when she started rolling out the problems with the items I had sent to her relative. I kept apologizing as she complained about each item. And then she said the dreaded words I would never forget, "I WILL NOT BE PAYING THE BALANCE BECAUSE I CAN'T SELL THIS."

I was sad. But quickly remembering I had not paid my staff, I switched to being defensive. I began to make excuses about the fact that it was a short period for production, and continued to blame external issues. I don't remember the specific moment I switched to begging; but I started begging her because I had not paid my staff for the job they had done and that meant this whole deal was now a loss!

I was thinking, How did I get here? From being enthusiastic about starting to export, to securing a paying customer, to her refusing to pay me what she owed me? Looking back now, I can advise my younger self and you if you're just starting out.

You must put structures from order inquiry to delivery of goods in place. Don't leave any touch point in place and don't cut corners. When accepting orders, ensure you send samples to the customer once, even if it is 10 pieces; start excellence from the days of small beginnings so you can imbibe that as a culture when you are much bigger.

I took that for granted when negotiating my prices at the time, but that was the beginning of my loss. I accepted a job, gave a unit cost and designs that were not mine, when I could have had a meeting with the manufacturers to arrive at a unit cost and whether the design would be possible within the timeline given to me.

Fulfilling an order is not the goal. Fulfilling the order excellently that you get a referral is the goal. So, you must do all to ensure the process is seamless and professional for your sake especially. Document everything so it can be referred to later, not WhatsApp messages that can disappear anytime with no traces of the conversation.

Avoid making commitments or stating prices via telephone calls with your customers. Use emails as a means of correspondence so you can keep track of what was agreed. If you're a supplier, not a manufacturer, always carry them along in the demands being made by the customer.

Likewise, if you are a manufacturer dealing with a customer directly, always ensure you are giving up-to-date information. This means that you speak to your production team before committing on an order, ensure logistics are in place, and do not start a production for an order not confirmed by payment even from existing clients; don't assume they can't ever owe you. They can.

I will continue with the customer story in the second edition of this book and I'll tell you how we resolved not paying me; you won't believe the way things ended. I will also explain why I shouldn't have stopped at an apology but offered solutions for both of us.

I have learnt so many more things I will be sharing, beyond the books I write on export, through the Borderless Trade Masterclass Series on pivotal parts in the export business. Things like creating your export plan, choosing a freight forwarder, export documentation and procedures which are usually a headache for most people. But I love the process and am always happy to help those who need guidance in that problem area.

The main lessons I want to highlight in the story I shared are these: put the right structures in place at every customer touchpoint. Do not assume the way you run your current business will suffice for international trade; it may not. You will need to upgrade your existing business systems and structures.

Also, don't let the passion or enthusiasm of earning in foreign currency push you to accepting what will not profit you or leave a bad taste in the mouth of an international buyer. Take the right path and you will get the right results.

I'm not asking you to know everything before you start. I'm asking you to be as prepared as possible.

Chapter Five

Frequently Asked Questions

Do I have to be a manufacturer before I can export? No. There are different types of exporters as mentioned in the beginning. A merchant exporter is a person engaged in trading activity and exporting or intending to export goods. Merchant exporters procure materials from a manufacturer and exports in his firm's name.

If you are good at sourcing for goods and getting them at very low prices, you can repackage and go on to resell on global online marketplaces. This is typically the case on some popular marketplaces where goods are shipped from the United States but the country of origin and production is in China.

The merchant has sourced for cheap and yet market standard products and repackaged it with a healthy profit margin.

You can also be a manufacturer exporter. This is a person who manufactures goods and exports or intends to export such goods. You also have Commodity exporters. These make up emerging markets and developing economies for which gross exports of commodities constitute at least 35 percent of total exports.

Commodity exporters are usually found in countries with large deposits of natural resources or large amounts of farmland, with populations too small to use up all their own resources. The trade of many commodity exporters is dominated by a single commodity. Most least developed countries are reliant on agricultural exports.

Yes, you can be a cross between all three categories if you have the capacity and infrastructure to handle it all.

HOW DO I TRANSPORT MY FINISHED GOODS?

In the second edition of this book, soon to be released, I talk extensively on transporting your finished goods and what you need to know about logistics and freight. There are different modes of transportation. Once your goods are ready to ship, you can ship by sea, air, road.

When you're starting out, I would strongly advise you hire a freight forwarder. A freight forwarder is a company that specializes in arranging the transportation of goods.

A freight forwarder can be hired by either the buyer or the seller in an international transaction, and they may pro-vide additional services such as packaging, document preparation, customs clearance.

Below is a trusted directory for airfreight suppliers. All you have to do is type in which country you are interested in. For example, for a list of airfreight suppliers in the United Kingdom, this would be -

https://azfreight.com/country/united-kingdom/

IS THERE A COMPANY THAT CAN HELP WITH END-TO-END EXPORT DOCUMENTATION AND PROCEDURE FOR ME?

Yes. There are companies that offer to take the burden off you in export documentation; from drafting customs documents to ensuring your package arrives on time, experts can provide the peace of mind you need so you can focus on the more important things.

In some cases, some of these companies go an extra mile by offering other services such as market research, export training for companies, consultancy on international trade. An example of such an organization is a company located in Nigeria: XPT LOGISTICS INTERNATIONAL LTD. Their services offered include but are not limited to:

- Market Penetration In The Region And Beyond: Providing market research and survey, conducting market intelligence for companies, and assessing product potential in the West African region and beyond.

- Export Logistics: Specialising in export freight forwarding processes and documentation, trade experts on custom reforms and regulations.
- Export Consultant: Providing consultancy services on international trade.

I FEEL SO OVERWHELMED. WHERE DO I START MY MARKET RESEARCH?

I understand that starting out on your export journey can feel overwhelming. You may be wondering, How do I start?

The easy answer is just start. Like I stated previously, conduct a secondary research first where you research the market first then the product you want to export, and its demand in the export destination.

Click the link below to begin your search for more question-specific research –

https://opentoexport.com/steps/selecting-a-market/

WHAT CAN I START EXPORTING? ARE THERE POPULAR PRODUCTS?

This is a common question; unfortunately, there is no straightforward answer. But I will do my best to break it down. Like I said, the first step, if you are looking to set up a new export business is to obtain market information.

The commercial success of export ventures relies on insightful understanding of the commodities in the export market. This encompasses trends, local competition, etc. So, the popularity list will vary from sector to sector.

For example, in Nigeria, there is no generic list. For agriculture, the common items for export are beans (dry), cocoa, ginger, sesame seeds, cashew nuts. Currently, main exports for raw cashew nuts are sent to Vietnam and India. There are opportunities for increasing the export of cashew kernels to other consumer markets, like Germany and Netherlands.

The estimated potential might very possibly increase further when the processing of cashew increases in Nigeria.

According to world top exports report, the following export product groups represent the highest dollar value in Nigerian global shipments during 2019. Also shown is the percentage share each export category represents in terms of overall exports from Nigeria.

1. Mineral fuels including oil: US$46.7 billion (87.1% of total exports)
2. Ships, boats: $3.2 billion (5.9%)
3. Other base metal goods: $2.1 billion (3.9%)
4. Cocoa: $311.1 million (0.6%)
5. Oil seeds: $299.7 million (0.6%)
6. Fertilizers: $151.7 million (0.3%)
7. Fruits, nuts: $113.4 million (0.2%)
8. Tobacco, manufactured substitutes: $103.7 million (0.2%)
9. Raw hides, skins (not fur skins), leather: $75.3 million (0.1%)
10. Aircraft, spacecraft: $69.8 million (0.1%)

IF I WANT TO START EXPORTING NOW, WHAT IS THE FIRST THING I MUST DO?

I get this question a lot, and the first I say is don't enter into this journey thinking you will start exporting or get your exporters certificate or license the day you decide.

The first thing to do is register as an exporter in your country. Start that process. There is a recognised national export agency appointed by the government in most countries.

Secondly, register for a program that offers 'zero-to-export' type training/seminar to get a broad overview of international trade processes.

The next step is to book a one-on-one consultation with an export trading consultant in your region to obtain an analysis of export related regulations and operational aspects that apply to your business.

WHEN I START MY EXPORT READINESS PROCESS, HOW SOON DO I GET MY FIRST ORDER?

This question is difficult to ascertain in terms of an exact timeline; but once you start your process of structuring your business for export, ensure you join export related associations, forums, schemes, trade fairs, and exhibitions.

Plug your business into export global conversations; whether online or in-person. Joining these associations is how you position your business for getting a piece of the $3 trillion pie in export.

Most international buyers would prefer going through trusted export trading platforms and export related agencies to get suppliers. You will wait longer to get an order if you go solo without any credibility as an export start-up.

For example, in Nigeria there are several export/manufacturing related agencies that are recognized by different countries. You can search further to learn more about them by typing their names into online search engines.

- Manufacturer's Association of Nigeria Export Promotion Group (MANEPG)
- Association of Nigeria-Asian Importers and Traders (ANIT)

- Association of Nigerian Exporters
- Africa Women's Entrepreneurship Program (AWEP)
- Nigeria Export Promotion Council
- The Nigeria Association of Chamber of Commerce
- Nigerian Textile Manufacturers of Association

This list can be generated for any other country also. Simply replace parts where Nigeria is mentioned with your country's name in the list above. I am sure similar results will pop up on the associations list relevant to you.

DO I NEED TO APPLY FOR LICENSES?

Yes. Even if you are starting with small quantities, it pays to align yourself with local regulations from the start. The export trading consultant/council in your country can help you with this application process.

WHERE SHOULD I BEGIN, NOW I HAVE THE INFORMATION I NEED?

Our advisors are standing by to coach you in the licensing and importation process. Remember, you aren't alone in this process and help is always available.

CLOSING WORDS

Exporting does not happen overnight. Building export readiness and successfully exporting may take months or even years to develop. A business pursuing exporting must be willing to commit the time and effort needed, while at the same time juggling domestic demands.

Preparation is key when you want to start your export journey. I cannot emphasize this enough. Attend trainings, webinars, and join forums that keep you in the loop about the export space. There is a lot to learn at the onset of an export journey: administrative procedures, distribution channels, standards and regulations, etc. It can be overwhelming.

Building export capacity and exporting takes time, money and patience. However, these challenges are not insurmountable, particularly to those who have prepared before engaging export markets. It's important to remember that being a big business is not a prerequisite to exporting. Size is not as important to export success as preparation is!

There will be costs involved in developing export markets for travel and communications, additional staff, or new marketing materials for example. It is also likely that the product selected for export may need to be customized to meet the requirements and expectations of the export market and may include labelling and packaging.

In order to export successfully, resource-scarce SMEs typically need to develop a broad range of skills in-house through training or hiring, or through outsourcing the skills that they do not have.

The expectations and norms around communication in many target markets are high. Customers and prospective customers must be able reach a business through multiple touch points, including email, web and social media; and businesses must be able to respond quickly to inquiries, even across time zones.

Exporting goods and services take different routes so learn the ropes of what applies to what you want to export. Take your time, do the necessary research. When you develop the export plan, implement it with your team fully on board.

Finally, seek expert help as you go along; you never really know it all because there's so much the export space has to offer your business; remember it's a global playing field.

Welcome to the big guys table. I wish you all the best as you take the first step.

See you in the second edition!

ABOUT THE AUTHOR

∽

OLORI BOYE-AJAYI is an experienced Business Strategist and Export Trading Consultant. With a Bachelor of Science degree in Business and Management from Bradford University School of Management, an MSc in Human Resource Management degree and extensive experience in management roles, Olori has developed strong competence in business development. She has comprehensive insight into the dynamics of the export trade, export ecosystem development, fashion trading, innovation, as well as community engagement and leadership.

She is Founder and Chief Operating Officer at The Katie Wang Company, a growing global fashion trading company with operations currntly in the U.K., Europe, Australia and the

US. The company operates as a social enterprise with expertise in the Apparel Industry and specific focus on design and development, manufacturing, supply chain, and small-scale retail business.

Spearheading the construction of the first technology-based manufacturing facility in West Africa, the Katie Wang Company is intentional about revolutionising the fashion space in Nigeria. The company prides itself on its core vision of linking talented fashion suppliers and manufacturers from Nigeria and other parts of Africa to global opportunities that improve their lives and their communities, multiple stitches at a time.

In her lead role, she designs and oversees the implementation of organisational strategy. She ensures that projects and operational practices align with international best practices while building the brand's positioning as a global influence within the fashion space. She manages revenue generation and corporate income targets together with overall business growth objectives.

With her involvement in the exportation industry, she has grown a passion for the exploration of Industrial Park Development within the Nigerian economic ecosystem. Prior to her pursuit of entrepreneurship and export value chain management, Olori worked as a Project Management Executive within the Human Resources industry.

Olori's devotion to excellence and the growth of the African economic ecosystem has been repeatedly recognised. In 2017, she was listed by SME 100 as one of the 'Top 100 Female Entrepreneurs in Nigeria' for her contribution to the Nigerian entrepreneurial ecosystem. In 2018, she received international recognition for her work and was nominated for the distinguished international fellowship program, the International Visitor Leadership Program (IVLP), which is run by the US State Department.

In 2019 she received the 'Distinguished Service Award' from the IVLP Alumni Association for her excellent contributions to the Secondary Schools Mentoring Programme which held in 2019. For her exemplary leadership and vision of elevating Africa's prosperity, she was awarded an honorary award in 2019 from the Fashion Development and Empowerment Center [AFDEC] for her contribution towards women empowerment in the Nigerian Fashion Industry.

Similarly, in 2019, she was honoured by Ideation Hub Africa for her tremendous contribution in using business as a driver of social change and nation building in Africa at the annual Women in Development Summit. In 2020, she was recognised as 'Leader and Mentor' for her role in the successful leadership and mentoring programs in Lagos state public schools by US Consulate General Public Affairs office, Lagos Nigeria.

Olori is passionate about community building and mentorship. She has volunteered as a mentor in several programmes within the WimBiz organisation as well as the Leading Ladies Foundation where she serves as a facilitator and a mentor for the free business workshops held frequently throughout the year. She also serves as a BSF Incubator Lead Facilitator which focuses on building competent business owners.

She is an Eloy Foundation mentor, and a leader and mentor within the IVLP Alumni network. She is also a speaker and trainer who has facilitated training for Women in Business at First City Monument Bank in the past and currently facilitates four-week classes every quarter teaching women in the Fashion and entrepreneurial space about structure, export readiness and export opportunities available at their current level. She is committed to using her platform to drive African development and women empowerment.

www.ingramcontent.com/pod-product-compliance
Lightning Source LLC
Chambersburg PA
CBHW070306220526
45465CB00004B/1770